# Bill Cosby
## Superstar

Patricia Stone Martin

illustrated by Bernard Doctor

Rourke Enterprises  Vero Beach, Florida

Manufactured in the United States of America

**Library of Congress Cataloging-in-Publication Data**

Martin, Patricia Stone.
  Bill Cosby – superstar

  (Reaching your goal biographies)
  Summary: a biography of a superstar – actor and
comedian Bill Cosby.
    1. Cosby, Bill, 1937-   – Juvenile literature.
2. Entertainers – United States – Biography – Juvenile
literature. 3. Comedians – United States – Biography –
Juvenile literature. [1. Cosby Bill, 1937-
2. Entertainers. 3. Afro-Americans – Biography] I. Title.
II. Series: Martin, Patricia Stone. Reaching your goal
biographies.
PN2287.C632M37 1987 792.7'028'0924 [B] [92] 87-12124
ISBN 0-86592-169-5

A nine-year-old boy sat on his front steps thinking. He wanted to help his mother. How could he earn money? What could he do? He looked around the yard and saw an orange crate. Then he looked at his shoes. Maybe he could shine shoes.

The boy turned the orange crate into a shoeshine box. He put black and brown polish into it. He put old rags into it. Then he went downtown. Some men stopped, and he shined their shoes. After they paid him, he ran home to show the money to his mother. She was very proud of him.

Today she has even more reasons to be proud of her son. He is a superstar!
His name is Bill Cosby.

William Henry Cosby, Jr., was born on July 12, 1937. His parents had three more boys after Bill. They were James, Russell, and Robert.

When Bill was nine years old, his father joined the navy and left home. Bill's mother went to work as a maid. Bill tried many jobs to help his mother. His very first job was shining shoes.

Bill had fun too. He had many friends. In the part of Philadelphia, Pennsylvania, where he grew up, there were not many yards. Bill and his friends played on the sidewalks and in the streets. They played baseball, football, and basketball. Bill was good at sports. He was also good at making jokes. He liked to make his friends laugh.

In high school, Bill was captain of the football team and captain of the track team. He didn't like to study. He would rather play sports. One teacher even said that Bill wanted to clown around more than study.

Soon Bill dropped out of school. He worked in a shoe repair shop. Then he worked in a car muffler plant. Bill did not like either job, so he joined the navy. While he was in the navy, he finished high school.

After four years in the navy, Bill went to Temple University in Philadelphia. This time he played sports *and* studied. He earned good grades. One summer he worked at a bar. He told jokes while he worked. People laughed. He told about his friend Fat Albert. Fat Albert weighed 2,000 pounds! He always said, "Hey, hey, hey!"

Bill told stories about other imaginary friends too. The owner of the bar offered him a job as a comedian. People loved listening to Bill, and Bill enjoyed hearing them laugh. He decided he had found what he wanted to do — make people laugh. He left Temple University to enter show business.

About this time, Bill met and married Camille Hanks. At first her parents were against the marriage. They weren't sure that Bill would be successful enough to support their daughter.

That same year, Bill was offered a role in "I Spy," a new TV show. Bill played the part of a tennis player who was really a spy. The show was a big hit, and Bill received an award for best actor.

After "I Spy," Bill starred in other TV shows. He also made records that were full of jokes, not music. He won another award for acting and won awards for his funny albums.

Bill also went back to college. He worked until he got the highest degree, a doctorate. He has earned the right to be called Dr. Cosby.

Bill likes teaching children. But he doesn't teach in schools. He teaches while he entertains. He made a record called *Bill Cosby Talks to Kids about Drugs*. Bill does not smoke or drink. He does not use drugs. He hopes children will not smoke, drink, or use drugs either. He knows that they can hurt people's lives.

Bill has been in several TV commercials. Almost everyone has seen him on TV *trying* to eat Jello pudding. The children with him take it away. Then they giggle.

Now Bill is starring in a popular TV series, "The Cosby Show." The show is about the Huxtable family. The children in the show are always having problems. The whole family solves the problems together. Funny things happen on the show every week. Bill hopes his TV show will help families. The Huxtables love and respect each other. Bill wants people to understand that this is the best way to live.

The Huxtable family is black. The things that happen in their family could happen in any family. Bill is trying to show that black people and white people are more alike than they are different.

In real life, Bill and Camille Cosby have five children. Their four girls are named Erika, Erinn, Ensa, and Evin. Their son is named Ennis. Bill's work keeps him away from home much of the time. He would like to spend more time with his family. He is a strict parent, but he is also a loving parent.

Bill Cosby has reached many of his goals. He makes people laugh. He has a good education. He has a happy family on TV. He has a happy family in real life. Bill still has goals ahead of him. He has already helped many children, and he hopes to help many more.

# Reaching Your Goal

What are your goals? Here are some steps to help you reach them.

1. **Decide on your goal.**
   It may be a short-term goal like one of these:
   learning to ride a bike
   getting a good grade on a test
   keeping your room clean
   It may be a long-term goal like one of these:
   learning to read
   learning to play the piano
   becoming a lawyer

2. **Decide if your goal is something you really can do.**
   Do you have the talent you need?
   How can you find out? By trying!
   Will you need special equipment?
   Perhaps you need a piano or ice skates.
   How can you get what you need?
   Ask your teacher or your parents.

**3. Decide on the first thing you must do.**
Perhaps this will be to take lessons.

**4. Decide on the second thing you must do.**
Perhaps this will be to practice every day.

**5. Start right away.**
Stick to your plan until you reach your goal.

**6. Keep telling yourself, "I can do it!"**

Good luck! Maybe someday you will become a superstar like Bill Cosby.

# Reaching Your Goal Books

**Beverly Cleary**
She Makes Reading Fun

**Bill Cosby** Superstar

**Jesse Jackson** A Rainbow Leader

**Ted Kennedy, Jr.**
A Lifetime of Challenges

**Christa McAuliffe**
Reaching for the Stars

**Dale Murphy**
Baseball's Gentle Giant

**Dr. Seuss** We Love You

**Samantha Smith** Young Ambassador

Rourke Enterprises, Inc.
P.O. Box 3328
Vero Beach, FL 32964